Fatimah's First Fasting Day

Mini Mu'min Du'a Series #5

www.Mini-Mumin.com

Copyright © 2012 Mini Mu'min Publications

All rights reserved. This publication may not be reproduced in whole or in part by any means whatsoever without written permission from the copyright owner.

Introduction

All praise is due to Allah the Most High, may Allah send His blessings on the Prophet Muhammad (saw), his family, his companions, and those who follow him in righteousness until the Day of Judgment.

"And remember your Lord by your tongue and within yourself, humbly and in awe, without loudness, by words in the morning and the afternoon, and be not among those who are neglectful." (Holy Qur'an 7:205)

The **Mini Mu'min Du'a Series** is designed to help you teach your child essential Islamic supplications and the situations in which they would be used. Each book focuses on a single topic, with key vocabulary highlighted. These key words can then serve as a tool to remind your child of important points. All supplications are shown in Arabic text, translation, and transliteration. For any assertions regarding fiqh we have provided textual proofs, from the Qur'an and authentic Sunnah of the Prophet (saw), at the bottom of the relevant page. Each story is accompanied by original artwork, but in accordance with Islamic beliefs we do not use human or animal images.

Transliteration has been provided here as a means to help those who do not know Arabic to teach supplications to their children. But it must be noted that all transliteration is imperfect and cannot accurately represent Arabic sounds in their entirety. We therefore encourage anyone who uses our books to use the transliteration as a tool, but not an end in itself, and to eventually learn the supplications in the original Arabic.

In some cases, sounds will be represented in the transliteration (because they are present in the Arabic text) that will not actually be pronounced. These generally occur at the end of a supplication and are related to the Arabic rules for pausing and stopping. To clarify this for non-Arabic speakers, we have placed brackets [ ] around those sounds in the transliteration that would not be pronounced when reciting the supplication.

Thank you for purchasing this book, may Allah benefit both you and your child through it, forgive us for any errors we have made, and benefit us in this life and the Hereafter if there is any good in it.

"O you who believe! Fasting has been made obligatory upon you just as it was made obligatory upon those who were before you, so that you may have Taqwa (piety)"

(Holy Qur'an 2:183)

Fatimah,
like many other Muslim children,
(Maybe a child just like you!)

Is finally old enough to do something
She has always wanted to do…

The month of Ramadan is almost here,
And it will be more special than the last,

Because this will be the very first year,
That Fatimah is going to fast!

Fatimah knows that **Ramadan starts**,
With the **sighting of the new moon**.[1]

She has been keeping track of the days,
And knows it should appear very soon.

So, like Muslims all around the world,
She looks up, watching the fading sun,

Waiting for the sign that will tell them,
The month of Ramadan has begun!

---

[1] Narrated Ibn 'Umar (ra): I heard Allah's Messenger (saw) saying, "When you see the crescent (of the month of Ramadan), start observing *Saum* (fast), and when you see the crescent (of the month of Shawwal), stop observing *Saum* (fast); and if the sky is overcast (and you can't see it) then regard the crescent (month) of Ramadan (as of 30 days)." (Al-Bukhaari 3/124)

As the new moon rises,
Muslims everywhere gaze up in delight…

It is the **new moon of Ramadan**,
And this, the first of its many
blessed nights!

Those who have the joy of seeing it,
Tell those who did not yet hear.[2]

Happy greetings fly around the world,
To every corner far and near!

---

[2] Narrated Ibn 'Umar (ra): The people tried to sight the moon, so I informed the Messenger of Allah (saw) that I had sighted it, so he fasted and commanded the people to fast. (Abu Dawud 13/2335, Al-Albaani graded it as "Sahih" in his *Sahih Sunan Abi Dawud* 2/2342)

Note: This is proof that **one** reliable witness is sufficient to determine the beginning of fasting for the month of Ramadan. **Two** reliable witnesses are required for sighting the Eid crescent, this ruling is the consensus. (See *Bulugh Al-Maram* pg. 227 footnote #2)

When Fatimah saw the new moon,
She knew exactly what to do—

She made du'a right away,
Just as her parents had taught her to…

Du'a for Sighting a New Moon

اللهُ أَكْبَرُ، اللَّهُمَّ أَهِلَّهُ عَلَيْنَا بِالأَمْنِ وَ الإِيمَانِ، وَ السَّلَامَةِ وَ الإِسْلَامِ، وَ التَّوْفِيقِ لِمَا تُحِبُّ وَ تَرْضَى، رَبُّنَا وَ رَبُّكَ اللهُ

"Allaahu Akbar, Allaahumma ahillahu 'alayna bil-amni wal-eemaan[i], wassalaamati wal-Islaam[i], wattawfeeqi limaa tuhibbu wa tardhaa, Rabbunaa wa Rabbukallaah[u]."

(Allah is the Most Great. O Allah, bring us the new moon with security and faith, with peace and in Islam, and in harmony with what You love and what pleases You. Our Lord and your Lord is Allah.[3])

---

[3] (At-Tirmidthi and Ad-Darimi, see also: *Kalimat-Tayyib* #161, Hadith Sahih) Note: This is a general supplication for any new moon, not only that of Ramadan.

Fatimah was SO excited,
She felt like a balloon ready to POP!

After Maghrib she started asking questions,
About everything, she just couldn't stop…

"Baba,[4] tell me all about fasting,"
Said Fatimah, "I really want to learn,

Tell me why it is super important and
About all the good deeds that I can earn!"

---

[4] "Baba" -Arabic word meaning "Father"

"Allah gave us fasting," he began,
"As way to make our **goodness grow**,[5]

And a special way to **worship** Him,
Inside ourselves, that only He can know.[6]

Fasting is a big part of our lives,
And every Muslim holds it very dear.

In fact, fasting is SO important in Islam,
We fast for a **whole month** in every year."

---

[5] "O you who believe! Fasting has been made obligatory upon you just as it was made obligatory upon those who were before you, so that you may have Taqwa (piety)" (Holy Qur'an 2:183)

[6] Narrated Abu Huraira (ra): Allah's Messenger (saw) said, "... (Allah says about the fasting person), 'He has left his food, drink, and desires for My sake. The *Saum* (fast) is for Me'... " (Al-Bukhaari 3/118)

Note: "Although all practices of worshipping are for Allah, here Allah singles out *Saum* (fast) because *Saum* (fast) cannot be practiced for the sake of showing off as nobody can know whether one is observing *Saum* (fast) or not, except Allah. Therefore, *Saum* (fast) is a pure performance that cannot be blemished with hypocrisy." (*Fath Al-Bari*, Vol. 5, Page 10)

"You know Islam is built on **five pillars**,[7]"
He said, "can you tell me the whole list?"

"Shahada, Salaat, Zakaat, Hajj, Saum…"
She replied, "Is there anything I missed?"

"Alhamdu lillah!" replied her father,
"You remembered every single one!

Saum is when we fast in **Ramadan**,[8]
Every day, until the month is done."

---

[7] Narrated Ibn 'Umar (ra): Allah's Messenger (saw) said, "Islam is based on (the following) five (principles): To testify (Shahada) that none has the right to be worshipped but Allah and Muhammad is the Messenger of Allah, to offer the (compulsory congregational) prayers (Salaat) dutifully and perfectly, to pay Zakaat (obligatory charity), to perform Hajj (pilgrimage to Mecca), and to observe Saum (fast) during the month of Ramadan." (Al-Bukhaari 1/7)

[8] "The month of Ramadan in which was revealed the Qur'an, a guidance for mankind and clear proofs for the guidance and the criterion (between right and wrong). So whoever of you sights (the crescent on the first night of) the month (of Ramadan, i.e. is present at his home), he must observe *Saum* (fast) that month…" (Holy Qur'an 2:185)

"Muslims **must** fast in Ramadan," he said,
"Because fasting in this month is **fard**.[9]

But Allah knows that for some people,
This task would be much too hard.

Children do not have to fast at all,[10]
Until they are old enough-
just like you!

For the **old**, or those who **cannot fast**,
Feeding the poor is all they have to do.[11]"

---

[9] "Fard"- Arabic word meaning "obligatory" (See footnote #5)

[10] Narrated Aisha (raa): The Messenger of Allah (saw) said, "There are three (persons) whose actions are not recorded: a sleeper till he awakes, an idiot till he is restored to reason, and a child till he reaches puberty." (Abu Dawud 38/4384, Al-Albaani graded it "Sahih" in his *Irwaa' Al-Ghaleel* 2/297)

[11] Narrated 'Ata: That he heard Ibn 'Abbas (ra) reciting the Divine Verse: '*And for those who can fast with difficulty they have (a choice either fast or) to feed a poor (person) (for every day)...*' (2:184) Ibn 'Abbas said, "This verse is not abrogated, but it is meant for old men and old women who have no strength to fast, so they should feed one poor person for each day of fasting (instead of fasting)." (Al-Bukhaari 60/32) Note: This allowance for giving charity and not making up the missed days is for the elderly and those who are ill, **if they are not expected to recover from their illness**. If the one who is ill **recovers and is able to fast**, then making up the missed fasts is required. (See *Minhaj Muslim*, Vol. 2, Page 91)

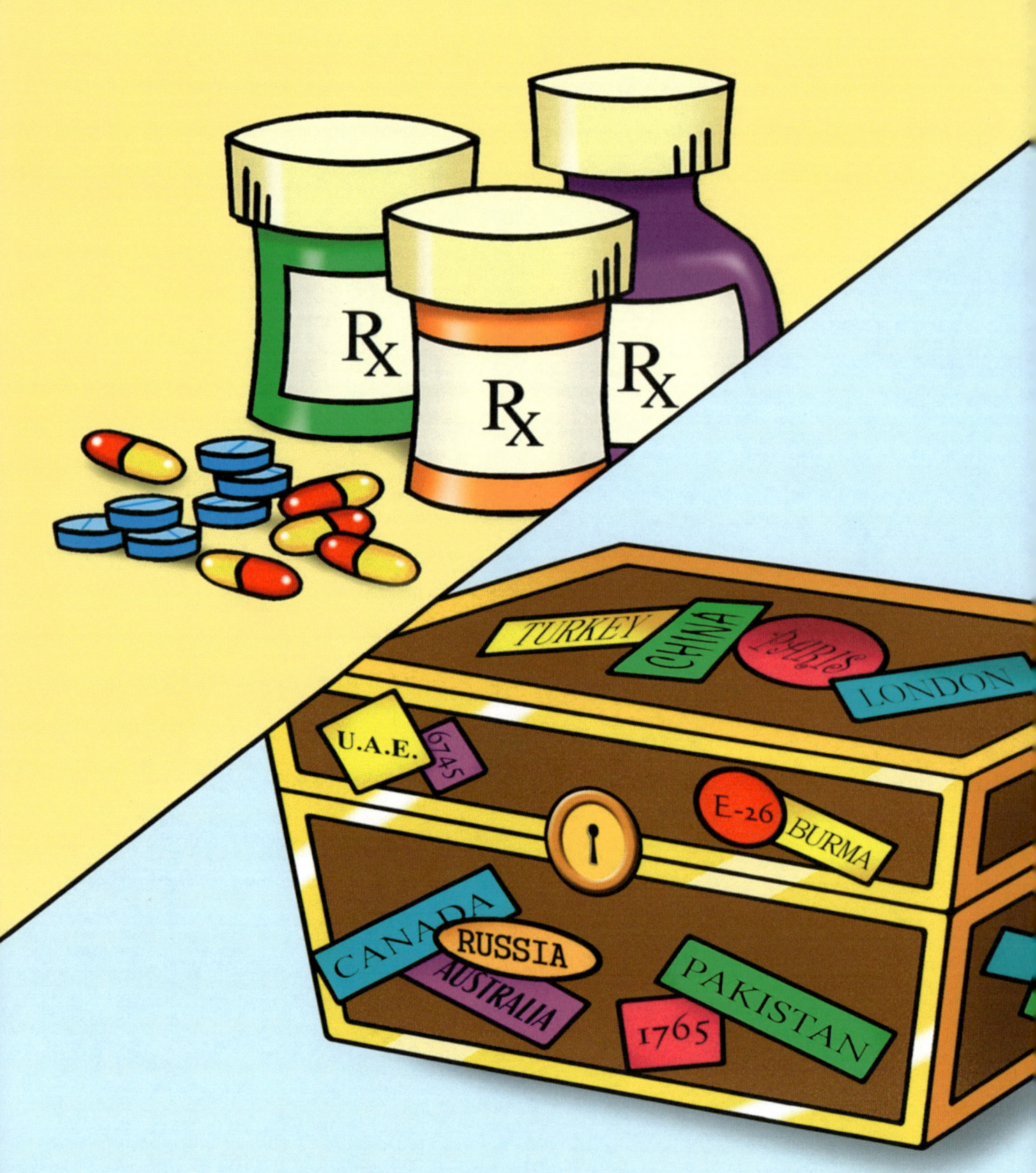

"But what if you are **sick**, or too **weak**,"
Asked Fatimah, "or **traveling** far away?"

"You can **choose not to fast** right now,[12]"
He replied, "and **make it up** another day."

"But when you are old enough and able,"
He added, "your fasting <u>must</u> begin.

Not fasting when you can do it easily,
Is indeed a very great sin."

---

[12] "…and whoever is ill or on a journey, the same number [of days which one did not observe *Saum* (fasts) must be made up] from other days…" (Holy Qur'an 2:185)

Narrated Anas bin Malik (ra): We used to travel with the Prophet (saw) and neither did the fasting persons criticize those who were not fasting, nor did those who were not fasting criticize the fasting ones. (Al-Bukhaari 3/168)

Note: This allowance to choose to fast, or to choose not to fast and make up missed days later, is for the traveler and the one who is ill and **expects to recover** from his illness (for those who **do not expect to recover** see footnote #11). Also included in this allowance is the pregnant or nursing mother, if she fears for herself or her infant. (See *Minhaj Muslim,* Vol. 2, pg. 90-91)

"Now, it's YOUR turn," said her father,
"I have a few questions for you, too…

What does 'fasting' mean?
When you fast, what do you have to do?"

"That's easy!" said Fatimah with a grin,
"**No drinking** while the **sun is up.**[13]

Not even a sip or a swallow-
Not even the tiniest cup!"

---

[13] "…eat and drink, until the white thread (light) of dawn appears to you distinct from its black thread (darkness of night); then complete your *Saum* (fast) till the nightfall…" (Holy Qur'an, 2:187)

Narrated 'Adi bin Hatim (ra): When the following verses were revealed: *'Eat and drink until the white thread appears to you, distinct from the black thread…'* I took two (hair) strings one black and the other white, and kept them under my pillow and went on looking at them throughout the night but could not make anything out of it. So, the next morning I went to Allah's Messenger (saw) and told him the whole story. He explained to me, "That verse means the darkness of night and the whiteness of dawn." (Al-Bukhaari 3/140)

"AND…" she continued carefully,
"**No eating** while there is **daylight**,[14]

You can't eat anything at all-
Not even a nibble or a bite!"

"What if you **forget**," her father asked,
"And eat something, what should you do?"

"**Keep on fasting**," answered Fatimah,
"Because Allah is the one who fed you![15]"

---

[14] "…eat and drink, until the white thread (light) of dawn appears to you distinct from its black thread (darkness of night); then complete your *Saum* (fast) till the nightfall…" (Holy Qur'an, 2:187)

Note: There are additional prohibitions for adults; here our focus is on items relevant to children.

[15] Abu Huraira (ra) reported: Allah's Messenger (saw) as saying, "If anyone forgets (that he is fasting) and eats or drinks he should complete his fast, for it is only Allah who has fed him and given him drink." (Muslim 6/2575 and Al-Bukhaari 3/154)

"Subhaan-Allah![16]" he said proudly,
"You really know your stuff!

But don't forget-
Not eating and drinking alone,
isn't quite enough...

Be careful not to **lie** or **insult** others,
Or **argue** and go around being **mad**,

Or you'll lose the **reward** of your fasting,
For behaving in a way that is bad.[17]"

---

[16] "Subhaan-Allah" - An Arabic phrase meaning "Glory be to Allah!"

[17] Narrated Abu Huraira (ra): The Prophet (saw) said, "Whoever does not give up lying speech (false statements) and acting on those lies and evil actions etc., Allah is not in need of his leaving his food and drink [i.e. Allah will not accept his *Saum* (fast)]." (Al-Bukhaari 3/127)

Note: These kinds of actions decrease the **reward** of your fasting, but your fast is not technically invalidated, and no expiation or making up of the fasting day is required.

Fatimah looked a bit worried,
"So, getting angry could ruin my fast?

What if someone is being mean to me,
What can I do?" she finally asked.

"Say '**I am fasting**',[18]" her father replied,
"That was Rasulullah's (saw) advice...

After all, to get the reward of fasting,
Keeping your temper is a very small price!"

---

[18] Narrated Abu Huraira (ra): Allah's Messenger (saw) said, "Allah said, '*All the deeds of Adam's sons (people) are for them, except fasting which is for Me, and I will give the reward for it.*' fasting is a shield or protection from the Fire and from committing sins. If one of you is fasting, he should avoid relations with his wife and quarreling, and if somebody should fight or quarrel with him, he should say, '*I am fasting.*' By Him in Whose Hands my soul is the unpleasant smell coming out from the mouth of a fasting person is better in the sight of Allah than the smell of musk. There are two pleasures for the fasting person, one at the time of breaking his fast, and the other at the time when he will meet his Lord; then he will be pleased because of his fasting."
(Al-Bukhaari 31/128)

"Fasting," he explained kindly,
"Is a thing between **you** and your **Lord**,

He is the one who will decide,
How much will be your **reward**.[19]

Maybe you will earn a little…
Or maybe you will earn a lot…

It all depends on **HOW** you fasted,
And only Allah knows what you got."

---
[19] See footnote #18

Fatimah's mother added thoughtfully,
"Subhaan-Allah, that is so true!

There are so many rewards and benefits
That fasting can bring to you."

"What do you mean?" inquired Fatimah,
"I thought good deeds were all you get?"

"Oh no!" she replied with a smile,
"That is only the beginning…
we're not nearly done yet!"

"Think about the smell," she began,
"Of the <u>best</u> perfume you've ever known…

Well, did you know that we smell good,
When we fast for Allah alone?

He loves it so much when we fast,
From before dawn until the dusk,

That the **smell of our breath**,[20] to Allah
Is **better than the smell of musk!**"

---

[20] See footnote #18

"That is truly fantastic!" said her father,
"But there's yet another benefit for you…

When you fast each and every year,
You get rid of your bad deeds, too!

All the **small sins** that you committed,
Between this Ramadan and the last…

Are **forgiven**,[21] as a special reward,
For those completed fasts!"

---

[21] Abu Huraira (ra) reported: that the Messenger of Allah (saw) said, "The five (daily) prayers and one Friday prayer to (the next) Friday prayer and Ramadan (fasting) to the next Ramadan (fasting) are expiation for whatever was between them (of sins), as long as the major sins are avoided." (Muslim 2/450)

Narrated Abu Huraira (ra): Allah's Messenger (saw) said, "Whoever observes fasts during the month of Ramadan out of sincere faith, and hoping to attain Allah's rewards, then all his past sins will be forgiven." (Al-Bukhaari 2/37)

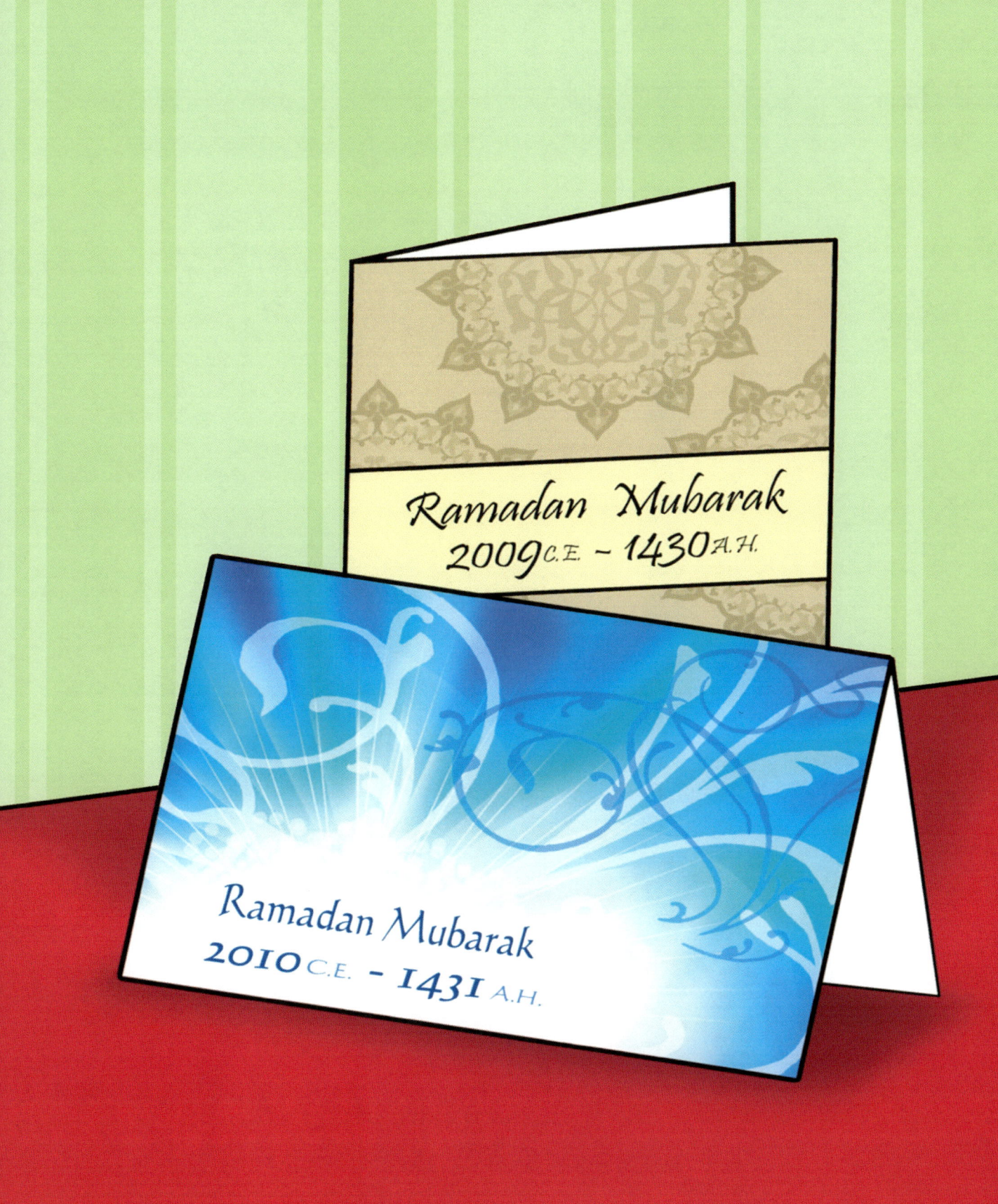

IN THIS LIFE...

BAD DEEDS

FASTING IS A SHIELD

HELLFIRE

...AND THE NEXT

"That is wonderful!" said her mother,
"But there's more you get when you fast,

I can tell you something else,
Even more amazing than the last…

In this life, fasting is a **shield**,[22]
Against **doing things you shouldn't do**,

and…

In the Hereafter, fasting is a **shield** again,
And protection from the **Hellfire** for you!"

---

[22] See footnote #18

"That is marvelous!" said her father,
"But I know something even more nice…

Did you know for the fasting people,
There is a special **gate in Paradise**!

On the Day of Judgment,
The people will be called to come,

Only the **ones who fasted** can enter
The gate of **Ar-Raiyan**,[23] not just anyone."

---

[23] Narrated Sahl (ra): The Prophet (saw) said, "There is a gate in Paradise called *Ar-Raiyan*, and those who observe *Saum* (fasts) will enter through it on the Day of Resurrection and none except them will enter through it. It will be said, 'Where are those who used to observe *Saum* (fasts)?' They will get up, and none except them will enter through it. After their entry the gate will be closed and nobody will enter through it." (Al-Bukhaari 3/120)

"Now that I know the rewards of fasting,"
Said Fatimah, "I can hardly wait to start!"

"Just remember," said her mother,
That fasting **begins** in your **heart**...

This is your first time fasting
And you want to start out right-

So, if you want to fast **tomorrow**,
You have to make your **niyyah**[24] **tonight**!"

---

[24] "Niyyah"- An Arabic word meaning "intention". Here it refers to making intention (mentally) to fast the next day, no verbal statement is required.

Narrated 'Umar bin Al-Khattab (ra): I heard Allah's Messenger (saw) saying, "The reward of deeds depends upon the intentions and every person will get the reward according to what he has intended. So whoever emigrated for worldly benefits or for a woman to marry, his emigration was for what he emigrated for." (Al-Bukhaari 1/1)

Narrated Hafsa (raa): The Prophet (saw) said, "One who does not plan (intend) to fast during the night, there is no fast for him." (Abu Dawud 2454, and Al-Albaani graded it as "Sahih" in his *Irwaa' Al-Ghaleel* 4/914) Note: this is for obligatory fasts only, in a non-obligatory fast the intention can be made on the same day as fasting. (See *Minhaj Muslim,* Vol. 2, pg. 93)

Fatimah was learning so many things,
That she never knew before!

She had known fasting was important,
But now she saw it was so much more!

That night, Fatimah made her **intention**,
To fast tomorrow, and went right to bed.

She drifted off into peaceful sleep,
As thoughts of fasting filled her head…

Then, in the **early morning**,
Not at Fajr but a little bit before,[25]

Fatimah got up to get the **blessings**
Of having a special meal called '**Suhur**'.[26]

Her family gathered together to eat,
Her favorite- fried eggs and toast with jam!

"Are you ready to fast?" her father asked,
Fatimah smiled, "Insha-Allah, I am!"

---

[25] Narrated Anas (ra): Zaid bin Thabit (ra) said, "We took the '*Suhur*' (the meal taken before dawn while fasting is observed) with the Prophet (saw) and then stood up for the (morning) prayer." I asked him how long the interval between the *Suhur* and the Adhaan? He replied, "The interval was sufficient to recite fifty verses of Qur'an." (Al-Bukhaari 3/144)

[26] Narrated Anas bin Malik (ra): The Prophet (saw) said, "Take *Suhur* as there is a blessing in it." (Al-Bukhaari 3/146) Note: *Suhur* is not obligatory; it is from the Sunan (recommended acts) of fasting.

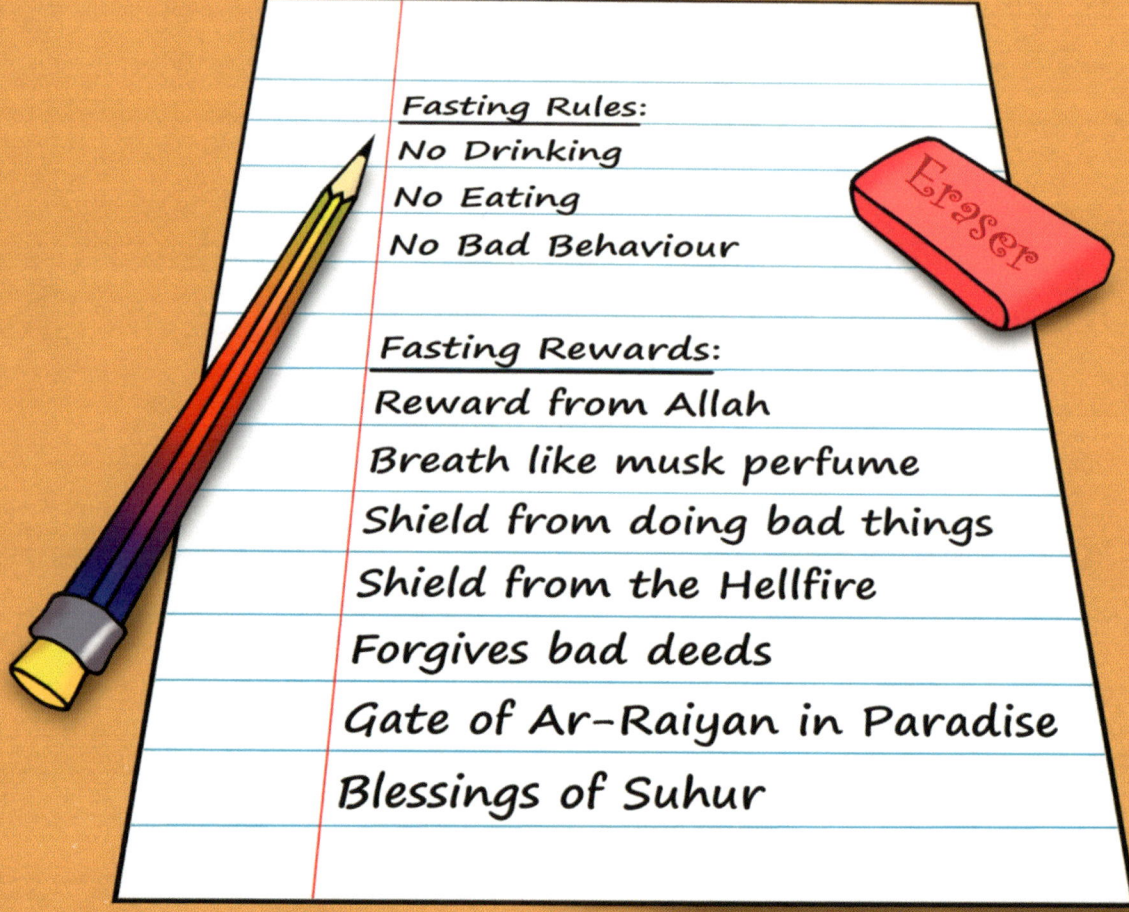

Her first fasting day started out easy,
But then again, she wasn't finished yet.

She kept reminding herself of all the rules,
No eating or drinking until sunset.

No bad behavior either,
Or she would lose and miss out,

On all the **rewards of fasting**,
That her parents had told her about.

As the sun blazed across the sky,
Fatimah was playing out in the yard.

She was getting pretty thirsty-
Suddenly, her fasting was becoming hard.

Then she heard a low grumble…
It was coming from her tummy.

She started to think of all the things
That she liked to eat that were yummy!

The day seemed to be getting longer,
Each minute slowly ticking past…

Fatimah realized that it wasn't so easy
As she had thought to complete her fast.

But then she reminded herself
That Allah's rewards are not for free.

"I have to work hard," she thought,
"If I want Allah to be pleased with me."

She went into the cool and shady house
And kept busy, helping her mother…

The time passed quickly as they worked,
Talking and laughing with each other.

"Don't worry," said her mother kindly,
"Soon enough it will be time for **Iftar**.[27]

Did you know that **breaking your fast**,
Is sort of like driving a car?"

---
[27] "Iftar"- An Arabic word referring to the breaking of the fast at sunset.

"If you are driving along," she explained,
"And come to a traffic light that is red,

You always **stop** right away,
You don't keep going on instead!

It's the same when we are fasting,
And the **sun sets**, we don't wait,[28]

We always **break our fast right away**,
We don't ever break our fast late.[29]"

---

[28] Note: The fast is broken at sunset, but before praying Maghrib (see footnote #31)

[29] "...eat and drink, until the white thread (light) of dawn appears to you distinct from its black thread (darkness of night); then complete your *Saum* (fast) till the nightfall..." (Holy Qur'an, 2:187)

Narrated Sahl bin Sad (ra): Allah's Messenger (saw) said, "The people will remain on the right path as long as they hasten the *Iftar* [breaking of the *Saum* (fast)]." (Al-Bukhaari 3/178)

Narrated 'Umar bin Al-Khattab (ra): Allah's Messenger (saw) said, "When night falls from this side and the day vanishes from this side and the sun sets, then the fasting person should break his fast." (Al-Bukhaari 31/175)

"Then, when it's time to break your fast,"
She continued, "what should you eat?"

"Oh!" said Fatimah excitedly,
"Can I have cookies as a special treat?"

"The best thing," she replied with a smile,
"For breaking your fast, are these two-

An odd number[30] of **dates** (**fresh** or **dry**),
Or some **water**- just a few sips will do.[31]"

---

[30] "It is recommended to break the fast with an **odd number** (of dates) –three, five, or seven…" (*Minhaj Muslim* Vol. 2, Page 94)

[31] Narrated Anas ibn Malik (ra): "The Messenger of Allah (saw) used to break his fast before praying (Maghrib) with some fresh dates; but if there were no fresh dates, he had a few dry dates, and if there were no dry dates, he took some mouthfuls of water." (Abu Dawud 13/2349, and Al-Albaani graded it as "Hasan Sahih" in his *Sahih Sunan Abi Dawud* 2/2356)

"After breaking your fast," she added,
"Make your du'a right away,

Always remember Allah,
And ask Him to accept your fasting
for that day."

Du'a Made After Breaking the Fast

ذَهَبَ الظَّمَأُ وَ ابْتَلَّتِ الْعُرُوقُ،
وَ ثَبَتَ الْأَجْرُ إِنْ شَاءَ الله

"*Thahabadh-dhama'u wabtallatil-'urooq[u], wa thabatal-ajru inshaa' Allaah[u].*"

(The thirst is gone,
the veins are moistened,
and the reward is confirmed,
if Allah wills.[32])

---

[32] (Abu Dawud, Al-Albaani graded it as "Hasan" in his *Sahih Sunan Abi Dawud* 2/2357 and *Irwaa' Al-Ghaleel* 4/920) Note: This du'a is said **after** breaking the fast, not before.

Before she knew it, the **sun was setting**-
Her first fasting day was complete!

For **Iftar**, she bit into a big plump **date**,
So delicious, so soft, and so sweet!

Then, Fatimah made her **du'a**,[33]
(The one we say when our fasting is done).

After **Maghrib**, her family sat down to eat,
Salad, fresh bread, and roasted meat
for everyone!

---
[33] See "Du'a Made After Breaking the Fast"

Now, Fatimah had the first joy
That we get when we finish our fast-

The **happiness** we feel at **Iftar** time,
Because we can eat and drink at last!

(Fatimah was certainly VERY happy
As she took a big bite of cake!)

But the greater **joy** will be to **meet Allah**,
If we fasted sincerely for His sake![34]

---
[34] See footnote #18

Other available titles in the Mini Mu'min Du'a Series:

Batool's Bedtime Story
Bilal's Bakery
Jameelah Gets Dressed
Muhammed Goes to the Masjid
Saliha Sneezes
Sheema's Shopping Spree
Waheeda the Wudoo' Wonder
Waleed Wakes Up

and many more!...

Visit our online bookstore at:

www.Mini-Mumin.com

Made in the USA
Charleston, SC
13 January 2014